PRTS

P9-ASG-126

#4718

BT
304.3
.B4
1981

A SHORT MEDITATION

ON THE MORAL GLORY

OF

THE LORD JESUS CHRIST

A

SHORT MEDITATION

ON

THE MORAL GLORY

OF

THE LORD JESUS CHRIST

BY

J. G. B.

John Gifford Bellett

BIBLE TRUTH PUBLISHERS
59 Industrial Road, P.O. Box 649
Addison, Illinois 60101

Printed in U.S.A.
1981

INTRODUCTION

It is the moral glory, or, as we speak, the character of the Lord Jesus, on which I meditate in these pages. All went up to God as a sacrifice of sweet savour. Every expression of Himself in every measure, however small, and in whatever relationship it was rendered, was incense. In His person (but surely there only) *man* was reconciled to God. In Him God recovered His complacency in man, and that too with unspeakable gain ; for in Jesus man is more to God than he would have been in an eternity of Adam innocency.

But in this Meditation on the Moral Glory of the Lord Jesus, it is most surely but a small part of that wondrous subject I affect to have reached. I may give occasion to fruitful thoughts in the souls of others, and that will be good.

The Lord's *Person* I assume—God and man in one Christ. His *work* I also assume ; that suffering service, or blood-shedding, accomplished on the Cross, whereby reconciliation is perfected, and wherein it is preached for the acceptance and joy of faith.

A SHORT MEDITATION

ON THE

MORAL GLORY OF
THE LORD JESUS CHRIST

"And when any will offer a meat-offering, his offering shall be of fine flour ; and he shall pour oil upon it, and put frankincense thereon ; and he shall bring it to Aaron's sons the priests ; and he shall take thereout his handful of the flour thereof, and of the oil thereof, with all the frankincense thereof ; and the priest shall burn the memorial of it upon the altar, to be an offering made by fire, of a sweet savour unto the Lord."—Lev. 2 : 1, 2.

THE glories of the Lord Jesus are threefold—personal, official, and moral. His personal glory He veiled, save where faith discovered it, or an occasion demanded it. His official glory He veiled likewise ; He did not walk through the land as either the divine Son from the bosom of the Father, or as the authoritative Son of David. Such glories were commonly hid, as He passed on in the circumstances of life day by day. But His moral glory could not be hid : He could not be less than perfect in every thing—it belonged to Him, it was Himself. From its intense excellency, it was too bright for the eye of man ; and man was under constant exposure and rebuke from it. But there it shone, whether man could bear it or not. It now illuminates every page of the four evangelists, as it once did every path which the Lord Himself trod on this earth of ours.

It has been said of the Lord—'His humanity was perfectly natural in its development'. This is very beautiful and true. Luke 2 : 52 would verify this. There was nothing of unnatural progress in him : all was orderly increase. His wisdom kept pace with His stature, or age. He was the child first, then the man. By-and-by, as a Man (God's man in the world), He will testify of the world that its works are evil and be hated by it ; but as a child (a child after God's heart, as I may say), He will be subject to His parents, and under the law, and as one perfect ; in such conditions He grew in favour with God and man.

But though there was *progress* in Him, as we thus see, there was no cloud, or perversion, or mistake ; in this He distinguished Himself from all. His mother pondered things in her heart ; but cloud and indistinctness, nay, darkness itself, beset her mind, and the Lord had to say to her, "How is it that ye sought me ?" But with Him, progress was but one form of moral beauty—His growth was orderly and was seasonable ; and, I may add, that as 'his humanity was perfectly natural in its development', so was His character entirely human in its expressions : all that displayed it was common to man, as I may say.

He was the tree planted by the rivers of water, that bringeth forth His fruit in His season (Psalm 1) ; and all things are only beautiful in their season. The moral glory of "the child Jesus" shines in its season and generation ; and when He became a Man, the same glory only gets other seasonable expressions. He knew when to own the claims of His mother, when she made them ; when to resist them, though she made them ; when to recognize them unsought (Luke 2 : 51, 8 : 21 ; John 19 : 27) ; and, as we afterwards track Him, He knew Gethsemane in season, or according to its character ; and the Holy Mount in its season, winter and summer, to His spirit. He knew the well of Sychar, and the road which led Him to Jerusalem for the last time. He trod each path, or filled each spot, in that mind that was according to the character it bore under God's eye. And so on occasions which called for still more energy. If it be the defilement of His Father's house, He will let zeal consume him ; if it be His own wrong at the hand of some Samaritan villagers, He will suffer it, and pass on.

And all was perfect in its *combinations*, as well as in its *season*. He wept as He was reaching the grave of Lazarus, though He knew that He carried life for the dead. He who had just said, "I am the resurrection and the life", wept. Divine power would leave human sympathies free to take their full course.

And it is assemblage, or combination of virtues, which forms moral glory. He knew, as the apostle speaks, "how to abound and how to be abased "; how to use moments of prosperity, so to call them, and also times of depression. For, in His passage through life, He was introduced to each of these.

Thus, He was introduced for a moment to His glory ; and a very bright moment it was. I allude to the trans-figuration. He was high in His honours there. As the sun, the source of all brightness, there He shone ; and such eminent ones as Moses and Elias are there, taking of His glory from Him, and in it shining with Him. But as He descended the hill, He charged those who had been with Him, "the eye-witnesses of his majesty", not to speak of it. And when the people, on His reaching the foot of the hill, ran to salute Him (Mark 9 : 15),—His person still reflecting, I believe, though faintly, the glory which it had lately borne,—He does not linger among them to receive their homage, but at once addresses Himself to His common service ; for He knew "how to abound". He was not exalted by His prosperity. He sought not a place among men, but emptied Himself, made Himself of no reputation, quickly veiled the glory that He might be the servant ; the *girded*, not the *arrayed* One.

And it was thus with Him a second time, after He had become the risen Jesus, as we may see in John 20. He is there in the midst of His disciples, in such a glorious character as man had never borne or witnessed, and never could. He is there as the conqueror of death, and the spoiler of the grave. But He is not there—though in such glories—to receive the congratulations of His people, as we speak, and as one naturally would, who was finding Himself returned to the bosoms of friends and kinsfolk, after toil, and danger, and victory. Not that He was indifferent to sympathy : He sought it in season, and felt the want of it when He did not get it. But He is now, risen from the dead, in the midst of His disciples, rather as a visitor for a day, than as in a triumph. He is rather teaching them *their* interest, and not displaying *His own*, in the great things which had just been accomplished.

This was using a victory indeed, as Abraham knew how to use his victory over the confederate kings—a harder thing, as some have said, than to gain it. This, again, was knowing "how to abound", how "to be full".

But He knew "how to be abased" also. Look at Him

with the Samaritan villagers in Luke 9. At the outset of that action, in the sense of His personal glory, He anticipated His being "raised up", as He actually was afterwards (see Mark 16 : 19 ; 1 Tim. 3 : 16 ; the Greek word is the same) ; and in the common, well-known style of one who would have it known that a person of distinction was coming that way, He sends messengers before His face. But the unbelief of the Samaritans changes the scene. They would not receive Him. They refused to cast up a highway for the feet of this glorious One, but forced Him to find out for Himself the best path He could, as the *rejected* One. But He accepts this place at once, without a murmur in His heart. He becomes again (borrowing the word from Matt. 2) the Nazarene, seeing He was refused as the Bethlehemite, and He fills this new character on this side of the Samaritan village, as perfectly as He had filled the other character on the other side of it.

Thus He knew "how to be abased", and just so do we again see Him in Matt. 21. He enters the city as Son of David. All that could set Him off in that dignity surrounds and accompanies Him. He is in His earthly honour now, as He has been in His heavenly glory on the holy hill. It was His without robbery ; and when the moment demanded it, He can wear it. But the unbelief of Jerusalem now, as the unbelief of Samaria before, changes the scene, and He who had entered the city as her King has to leave it, to seek a night's lodging, so to speak, where best He could find it. But there He is, outside Jerusalem, as before He had been outside the Samaritan village, knowing "how to be abased".

What perfection! If the darkness comprehend *not* the

light of His personal or official glory, His moral glory shall only find occasion to shine the brighter. For there is nothing in morals or in human character finer than this combination of willing degradation in the midst of men, and the consciousness of intrinsic glory before God. We see it in some of the saints beautifully. *Abraham* was a willing stranger in the midst of the Canaanites all his days, not having a foot of land, nor seeking to have it ; but when occasion served, he would take headship even of kings, conscious of his dignity in God's sight, according to God's own counsel. Jacob would speak of his pilgrimage, of his few and evil days, making himself nothing in the reckoning of the world ; but he would at the same moment bless him who at that time was the greatest man on the earth, conscious that, under God and before him, he was "the better", the greater man of the two.

David would ask for a loaf of bread, and ask for it without shame. But, with all that, he would accept the homage due to a king, receiving the tribute of his subjects, as in the person of Abigail. Paul was bound with a chain, a prisoner in the palace, and would speak of his bonds ; but at that same moment he would let the whole court and high estate of the Roman world know, that he knew himself to be the blest man, the only blest man, in the midst of them.

It is this combination of willing degradation before man, and conscious glory before God, that gets its highest, brightest, nay (when I consider who He was), its infinite illustration in our Lord.

And there is still further moral beauty in this knowing how to abound, and how to be abased, how to be full, and how to suffer need ; for it tells us that the heart of him who has learnt that lesson is upon *the end* of the journey, rather than upon the *journey itself*. If the heart be on the journey, we shall not like these accidents and difficulties, the rough places and the hilly places ; but if it be on the end, it will in proportion overlook such things. It is surely a secret rebuke to some of us to trace all this.

But there are other combinations in the Lord's character that we must look at. Another has said of Him, "He was the most gracious and accessible of men". We observe in His ways a tenderness and a kindness never seen in man, yet we always feel that He was "a stranger". How true this is! He was "a stranger here"—a stranger as far as *revolted man* was filling the place, but intimately near as far as *misery or need demanded Him*. The distance He took, and the intimacy He expressed, were perfect. He did more than look on the misery that was around Him, He entered into it with a sympathy that was all His own ; and He did more than refuse the pollution that was around Him,— He kept the very distance of holiness itself from every touch or stain of it. See Him as exhibiting this combination of distance and intimacy in Mark 6. It is an affecting scene. The disciples return to Him after a long day's service. He cares for them. He brings their weariness very near to Him. He takes account of it, and provides for it at once, saying to them, "Come ye yourselves apart into a desert place, and rest awhile". But, the multitude following Him, He turns with the same readiness to them, acquainting Himself with their condition ; and having taken knowledge of them, as sheep that had no shepherd, He began to teach them. In all this we see Him very near to the rising, varied need of the scene around Him, whether that need be the fatigue of the disciples, or the hunger and ignorance of the multitude. But the disciples soon resent His attention to the multitude, and move Him to send them away. This, however, will in no wise do for Him. There is immediate estrangement between Him and them, which shortly afterwards expresses itself by His telling them to get into the ship while He sent the multitude away. But this separation from Him only works fresh trouble for them. Winds and waves are against them on the lake ; and then in their distress He is again near at hand to succour and secure them!

How consistent in the combination of holiness and grace is all this. He is near in our weariness, our hunger, or our danger. He is apart from our tempers and our selfishness. His holiness made Him an utter stranger in such a polluted world ; His grace kept Him ever active in such a needy and afflicted world. And this sets off His life, I may say, in great moral glory ; that though forced, by the quality of the scene around Him, to be a lonely One, yet was He drawn forth by the need and sorrow of it to be the active One. And these activities were spent on all kinds of persons, and had therefore to assume all kinds of forms. Adversaries,— the people, a company of disciples who followed Him (the twelve), and individuals ; these kept Him not only in constant, but in very various activity ; and He had to know, as surely He did to perfection, how to answer every man. And beside all this, we see Him at times at the *table* of others ; but it is only that we may still notice further various perfection. At the table of the Pharisees, as we see Him occasionally, He is not adopting or sanctioning the family scene, but being invited in the character which He had already acquired and sustained outside, He is there to act in that character. He is not a guest simply, under the courtesy and hospitality of the master of the house, but He has entered in His own character, and therefore He can rebuke or teach. He is still the Light, and will act as the Light ; and thus He exposes darkness within doors as He did abroad. (See Luke 7, 11).

But if He thus entered the house of the Pharisee again and again, in the character of a *teacher*, and would then, acting as such, rebuke the moral condition of things which He found there, He entered the house of the publican as a Saviour. Levi made Him a feast in his own house, and set publicans and sinners in His company. This is, of course objected to. The religious rulers find fault, and then the Lord reveals Himself as a Saviour, saying to them, "They that be whole need not a physician, but they that are sick ; but go ye and learn what that meaneth, I will have mercy, and not sacrifice ; for I am not come to call the righteous, but sinners to repentance". Very simple, but very striking, and full of meaning, this is. Simon the Pharisee objected that a sinner should enter his house and approach the Lord Jesus ; Levi the publican provided such as these to be the fellow-guests of the Lord Jesus. And according to this, the Lord in the one house acts as a reprover, in the other, discloses Himself in the rich grace of a Saviour.

But we are to see Him at other tables still. We may visit him in Jericho and at Emmaüs. (See Luke 19 and 24). It was desire that received Him on each of these occasions ; but desire differently awakened—

awakened, I mean, under different influences. Zaccheus had been but a sinner, a child of nature, which is, as we know, corrupt in its springs and in its activities. But he had been just at that moment under the drawings of the Father, and his soul was making Jesus its object. He wished to see Him, and that desire being commanding, he had pressed his way through the crowd and climbed up into a sycamore tree, if he might but just see Him as He passed by. The Lord looked up, and at once invited Himself into his house. This is very peculiar,—Jesus is an uninvited, self-invited guest in the house of that publican at Jericho!

The earliest strivings of life in a poor sinner, the desire which had been awakened by the drawings of the Father, were there in that house ready to welcome Him ; but sweetly and significantly He anticipates the welcome, and goes in—goes in in full, consistent, responsive character, to kindle and strengthen the freshly-quickened life, till it break forth in some of its precious virtue, and yield some of its own good fruit. "Behold, Lord, the half of my goods I give to the poor ; and if I have taken any thing from any man by false accusation, I restore him fourfold". At Emmaüs *desire* had been again quickened, but under different conditions. It was not the desire of a freshly-drawn soul, but of restored saints. These two disciples had been unbelieving. They were returning home under a sorrow that Jesus had disappointed them. The Lord rebukes them shortly after He joined them on the road, but so orders His words as to kindle their hearts. When their walk together ends at the gate of their dwelling, the Lord makes as though He would go further. He would

not invite Himself as He had done at Jericho. They were
not in the moral state which suggested this, as Zaccheus
had been ; but, when invited, He goes in—goes in just to
kindle further the desire which had here invited Him—
to gratify it to the full. And so He does ; and they are
constrained by their joy to return to the city that night,
late as it was, to communicate it to their fellows.

How full of various beauty all these cases are! The
guest in the house of Pharisees, the guest in the house of
publicans, the guest in the house of disciples,—the invited
and the uninvited guest, in the person of Jesus, sits in His
place, in all perfection and beauty. I might instance Him
as a guest at other tables ; but, I will now look only at
one more. At Bethany we see Him adopting a family
scene. Had Jesus disallowed the idea of a Christian
family, He could not have been at Bethany, as we see He
was. And yet, when we get Him there, it is only some new
phase of moral beauty that we trace in Him. He is a
friend of the family, finding, as we find to this day among
ourselves, a home in the midst of them. "Now Jesus
loved Martha, and Mary, and Lazarus", are words which
bespeak this. His love to them was not that of a Saviour,
or a shepherd, though we know well He was each of these
to them. It was the love of a family friend. But though
a friend, an intimate friend, who might whenever He
pleased find a welcome there ; yet He did not interfere
with the arrangements of the house. Martha was the
housekeeper, the busy one of the family, useful and
important in her place ; and Jesus will surely leave her
where He finds her. It was not for Him to alter or settle
such matters. Lazarus may sit by the side of the guests

at the family table, Mary may be abstracted and withdrawn as in her own kingdom, or into the kingdom of God within her, and Martha be busy and serving. Be it so. Jesus leaves all this just as He finds it. He who would not enter the house of another unbidden, when entered into the house of those sisters and brother, will not meddle with its order and arrangements, and in full moral comeliness this is. But if one of the family, instead of carrying herself in her family place, step out of it to be a teacher in His presence, He must and will resume His higher character, and set things right *divinely*, though He would not interfere with or touch them *domestically*. (Luke 10).

What various and exquisite beauty! Who can trace all His paths? The vulture will have to say, it is beyond even the reach of his eye. And if no human eye can fully see the whole of this one Object, where is the human character that does not aid in setting off its light by its own shadows and imperfections? We none of us think of John, or of Peter, or of the rest of them, as hard-hearted or unkind. Quite otherwise. We feel that we could have entrusted them with our griefs or our necessities. But this little narrative in Mark 6, to which I referred, shows us that they are all at fault, all in the distance, when the hunger of the multitude appealed to them, threatening to break up their ease ; but, on the contrary, *that* was the very moment, the very occasion, when Jesus drew near. All this tells us of Him, beloved. 'I know no one', says another, 'so kind, so condescending, who is come down to poor sinners, as He. I trust His love more than I do Mary's, or any saint's ; not merely His power as God, but the tenderness of His heart as Man. No one

ever showed such, or had such, or proved it so well—none
has inspired me with such confidence. Let others go
to saints or angels, if they will ; I trust Jesus' kindness
more'. Surely, again I say, this is so—and this occasion
in Mark 6, betraying the narrow-heartedness of the best
of us, such as Peter and John, but manifesting the full,
unwearied, saving grace of Jesus, verifies it. But further :
there are in Him combinations of characters, as well as of
virtues or graces. His relationship to the world, when
He was here, exhibits this. He was at once a conqueror,
a sufferer, and a benefactor. What moral glories shine
in such an assemblage! He overcame the world, refusing
all its attractions and offers ; He suffered from it, witnessing for God against its whole course and spirit ; He
blessed it, dispensing His love and power continually,
returning good for evil. Its temptations only made Him
a conqueror ; its pollutions and enmities only a sufferer ;
its miseries only a benefactor. What a combination!
What moral glories shine in each other's company there!

The Lord illustrated that word that is among us, '*in*
the world, but not *of* the world'—a form of words which,
I suppose, has been derived from what He Himself says in
John 17 : 15 : "I pray not that thou shouldest take them
out of the world, but that thou shouldest keep them from
the evil". He illustrates this condition all through His
life ; for He was ever in the world, active in the midst of
its ignorance and misery, but never of it, as one that
shared its hopes or projects, or breathed its spirit. But
in John 7, I believe He is eminently seen in this character.
It was the time of the feast of tabernacles, the crowning
joyous time in Israel, the antepast of the coming kingdom,

the season of ingathering, when the people had only to *remember* that they had been in other days wanderers in a wilderness, and dwellers in a camp. His brethren propose to Him to take advantage of such a moment, when 'all the world', as we speak, was at Jerusalem. They would have Him make Himself important, make Himself, as we again speak, 'a man of the world'. "If thou do these things", they say, "show thyself to the world". He refused. His time had not then come to keep the feast of tabernacles. He will have His kingdom in the world, and be great to the end of the earth, when His day comes ; but as yet He was on His way to the altar, and not to the throne. He will not go to the feast to be *of* the *feast*, though He will be *in* it ; therefore when He reaches the city at this time, we see Him in *service* there, not in *honour*, not working miracles as His brethren would have had Him, that He might gain the notice of men ; but teaching others, and then hiding Himself under this, "My doctrine is not mine, but his that sent me".

Very peculiar and characteristic indeed all this is. And all this was some of the moral glory of the Man, the perfect Man, Jesus, in His relation to the world. He was a conqueror, a sufferer, and a benefactor—in the world, but not of it. But with equal perfectness do we see Him at times *distinguishing things*, as well as exhibiting these beautiful combinations. Thus, in dealing with sorrow which *lay outside*, as I may express it, we see tenderness, the power that relieved ; but in dealing with the trouble of *disciples*, we see faithfulness as well as tenderness. The leper in Matthew 8 is a stranger. He brings his sorrow to Christ, and gets healing at once. Disciples, in the same chapter, bring their sorrow also, their fears in the storm ; but they get rebuke as well as relief. "Why are ye fearful, O ye of little faith?" He says to them. And yet the leper had but little faith, as well as the disciples. If they said, "Lord, save us, we perish" ; he said, "Lord, if thou wilt, thou canst make me clean". But they are rebuked, while he is not, just because there was a different thing before the mind of the Lord, and justly so. It was *simply sorrow* in the one case ; it was *the soul as well as the sorrow* in the other. Tenderness, unmixed tenderness, was therefore His answer to the one ; faithfulness must form part of the other. The different relationship to Him, of disciples and strangers, at once accounts for this, and may show us how perfectly He distinguished things that came very near each other, but still were not the same. But further, as to this perfection. Though He Himself rebuke, He will not allow others lightly to do it. As in earlier days, Moses may be humbled by the Lord, but the Lord will not allow Miriam and Aaron to reproach him. (Num. 11 and 12). Israel in the wilderness will be chastened again and again by the hand of God, but in the face of Balaam, or any other adversary, He will be as one that has not seen iniquity in His people, and will not suffer any enchantment to prevail against them. So the Lord Jesus will beautifully and strikingly step in between the two disciples and the rebuking ten (Matt. 20.), and though He send a word of warning and admonition to John the baptist, as in secret (such a word as John's conscience alone might understand), He turns to the multitude to speak of John only with commendation and delight. And still further, as to this grace in distinguishing things that differ. Even in dealing with His disciples, there did come a moment when faithfulness can be observed no longer, and tenderness *alone* is to be exercised. I mean in the hour of parting, as we see in John 14 and 16. It was then 'too late to be faithful'. The moment would not have admitted it. It was a time which the *heart* claimed as entirely belonging to itself. The education of the soul could not go on then. He opens fresh secrets to them, it is true, secrets of the dearest and most intimate relationships, as between them and the Father ; but there is nothing that is to be called rebuke. There is no such word as, "O ye of little faith!" or "How is it that ye do not understand ?" A word that may sound somewhat like that is only the discharging of a wound which the heart had suffered, that they might know the love He had for them. This was the sacredness of the sorrow of a moment of parting, in the perfect mind and affection of Jesus ; and we practise it ourselves in some poor manner, so that we are at least able to enjoy and admire the full expression of it in Him. "There is a time to embrace", says the Preacher, "and there is a time to refrain from embracing". This is a law in the statute-book of love, and Jesus observed it.

But again. He was not to be drawn into softness, when the occasion demanded faithfulness, and yet He passed by many circumstances which human sensibilities would have resented, and which the human moral sense would have judged it well to resent. He would not gain His disciples after the poor way of amiable nature. Honey was excluded from the offerings made by fire as well as leaven. The meat offering had none of it (Lev. 2 : 11) ;

neither had Jesus, the true meat offering. It was not the merely civil, amiable thing that the disciples got from their Master. It was not the courtesy that consults for the ease of another. He did not gratify, and yet He bound them to him very closely ; and this is power. There is always moral power when the confidence of another is gained without its being sought ; for the heart has then become conscious of the reality of love. 'We all know', writes one, 'how to distinguish between love and attention, and that there may be a great deal of the latter without any of the former. Some might say, attention must win our confidence ; but we know ourselves that nothing but love does'. This is so true. Attention, if it be mere attention, is honey, and how much of this poor material is found with us! and we are disposed to think that it is all well, and perhaps we aim no higher than to purge out leaven, and fill the lump with honey. Let us be amiable, perform our part well in the civil, courteous, well-ordered social scene, pleasing others, and doing what we can to keep people on good terms with themselves, then we are satisfied with ourselves and others with us also. But is this service to God ? Is this a meat offering ? Is this found as part of the moral glory of perfect man ? Indeed, indeed it is not. We may naturally judge, I grant, that nothing could do it better or more effectually ; but still it is one of the secrets of the sanctuary, that *honey was not used to give a sweet savour to the offering.*

Thus, in progress, in seasonableness, in combinations, and in distinctions, how perfect in moral glory and beauty were all the ways of this Son of man!

The life of Jesus was the bright shining of a candle. It

was such a lamp in the house of God as needed no golden tongs or snuff-dishes. It was ordered before the Lord continually, burning as from pure beaten oil. It was making manifest all that was around, exposing and reproving ; but it ever held its own place uncondemned.

Whether challenged by disciples or adversaries, as the Lord was again and again, there is never an excusing of Himself. On one occasion disciples complain, "Master, carest thou not that we perish ?" But He does not think of vindicating the sleep out of which this challenge awakes Him. On another occasion they object to Him, "The multitude throng thee, and press thee, and sayest thou, Who touched me ?" But He does not need this inquiry, but acts upon the satisfaction of it. At another time Martha says to Him, "Lord, if thou hadst been here, my brother had not died". But He does not excuse His not having been there, nor His delaying for two days in the place where He was ; but instructs Martha in the *wondrous character which His delay had given to that hour*.

What a glorious vindication of His delay that was! And thus it was on every like occasion ; whether challenged or rebuked, there is never the recalling of a word, nor the retracing of a step. Every tongue that rises in judgment against Him, He condemns. The mother rebukes Him in Luke 2 ; but instead of making good her charge, she has to listen to Him convicting the darkness and error of her thoughts. Peter takes upon him to admonish Him : "This be far from thee, Lord ; this shall not be unto thee". But Peter has to learn, that it was Satan himself that in Peter prompted the admonition. The officer in the palace of the High Priest goes still further, correcting Him, and smiting Him on the cheek. But he is convicted of breaking the rules of judgment in the very face and place of judgment.

All this tells us of the way of the perfect Master. Appearances might have been against Him at times. Why did He sleep in the boat when winds and waves were raging ? Why did He loiter on the road when Jairus's daughter was dying ? or why did He tarry where He was when His friend Lazarus was sick in the distant village of Bethany ? But all this is but *appearance*, and that for a moment. We have heard of these ways of Jesus, this sleep, this loitering, and this tarrying, but we also see the end of Jesus, that all is perfect. Appearances were against the God of Job in patriarchal days. Messenger after messenger seemed too much, unrelenting, and inexorable ; but the God of Job had not to excuse Himself, nor has the Jesus of the evangelists.

Therefore, when we look at the Lord Jesus as the lamp of the sanctuary, the light in the house of God, we find at once that the tongs and snuff-dishes cannot be used. They are discovered to have no counterpart in Him. Consequently, they who undertook to challenge or rebuke Him when He was here had to go back rebuked and put to shame themselves. They were using the tongs or snuffers with a lamp which did not need them, and they only betrayed their folly ; and the light of this lamp shone the brighter, not because the tongs had been used, but because it was able to give forth some fresh witness (which it did on every occasion) that it did not need them.

And from all these instances we have the happy lesson, that we had better stand by, and let Jesus go on with His business. We may look and worship, but not meddle or interrupt, as all these were doing in their day—enemies, kinsfolk, and even disciples. They could not improve this light that was shining ; they had only to be gladdened by it, and walk in it, and not attempt to trim or order it. Let our eye be single, and we may be sure the candle of the Lord, set on the candlestick, will make the whole body full of light.

But I pass on. And I may further observe, that as He did not excuse Himself to the judgment of man in the course of His ministry, as we have now seen, so in the hour of His weakness, when the powers of darkness were all against Him, He did not cast Himself on the pity of man. When He became the prisoner of the Jews and of the gentiles, He did not entreat them or sue to them. No appeal to compassion, no pleading for life is heard. He had prayed to the Father in Gethsemane, but there is no seeking to move the Jewish high priest or the Roman governor. All that He says to man in that hour, is to expose the sin with which man, whether Jew or gentile, was going through that hour.

What a picture! Who could have conceived such an object! It must have been exhibited ere it was described, as has been long since observed by others. It was the perfect Man, who once walked here in the fulness of moral glory, and whose reflections have been left by the Holy Spirit on the pages of the evangelists. And next to the simple, happy, earnest assurance of His personal love to ourselves, (the Lord increase it in our hearts!) nothing more helps us to desire to be with Him, than this discovery of *Himself*. I have heard of one who, observing His bright and blessed ways in the four gospels, was filled with tears and affections, and was heard to cry out, 'O that I were with Him!'

If one may speak for others, beloved, it is this we *want*, and it is this we *covet*. We know our need, but we can say, the Lord knows our desire.

The same Preacher whom we quoted before, says, "There is a time to keep, and a time to cast away". (Eccles. 3 : 6). The Lord Jesus both kept and cast away, in the due season.

There is no waste in the services of the heart or the hand that worships God, be they as prodigal as they may. "All things come of thee", says David to the Lord, "and of thine own have we given thee".

The cattle on a thousand hills are His, and the fulness of the earth. But Pharaoh treated Israel's proposal to worship God as idleness, and the disciples challenge the spending of three hundred pence on the body of Jesus as waste. But to give the Lord His own, the honour or the sacrifice, the love of the heart, the labour of the hands, or the substance of the house, is neither idleness nor waste. It is chief work to render to God.

But here I would linger for a moment or two.

Renouncing Egypt is not idleness, nor is the breaking of a box of ointment on the head of Christ waste ; though we thus see, that a certain kind of reckoning among the children of men, and even at times (and that too frequent) among the saints of God, would charge these things as such. Advantages in life are surrendered, opportunities of worldly promise are not used, because the heart has understood the path of companionship with a rejected Lord.

But this is "idleness" and "waste," many will say : the advantages might have been retained by the possessor, or the opportunities might have been sought and reached, and then used for the Lord. But such persons know not. Station, and the human, earthly influence that attaches to it, is commended by them, and treated almost as "a gift to be used for profit, and edification, and blessing". But a rejected Christ, a Christ cast out by men, if known spiritually by the soul, would teach another lesson.

This station in life, these worldly advantages, these opportunities so commended, are the very Egypt which Moses renounced. He refused to be called the son of Pharaoh's daughter.

The treasures of Egypt were not riches in his esteem, because he could not use them for the Lord. And he went outside of them, and the Lord met him there, and used him afterwards, not to accredit Egypt and its treasures, but to deliver his people out of it.

I follow this a little here, for it is, I feel, important to us.

All this renunciation, however, must be made in the understanding and faith of a rejected Lord ; it will otherwise want all its fine, and genuine, and proper character. If it be made on a mere *religious* principle, as that of working out a righteousness or a title for ourselves, it may well be said to be something worse than idleness or waste. It then betrays an advantage which Satan has got over us, rather than any advantage we have got over the world. But if it be indeed made in the faith and love of a rejected Master, and in the sense and intelligence of His relation to this present evil world, it is worship.

To serve man at the expense of God's truth and principles is not christianity, though persons who do so will be called "benefactors". Christianity considers the glory of God, as well as the blessing of man ; but as far as we lose sight of this, so far shall we be tempted to call many things waste and idleness which are really holy, intelligent, consistent, and devoted service to Jesus. Indeed, it is so. The Lord's vindication of the woman who poured her treasure on the head of Jesus tells me so. (Matt. 26). We are to own God's glory in what we do, though man may refuse to sanction what does not advance the good order of the world, or provide for the good of our neighbour. But Jesus would know God's claims in this self-seeking world, while He recognised (very surely, as we may know) His neighbour's claim upon Himself.

He knew when to cast away, and when to keep. "Let her alone," He said of the woman who had been upbraided for breaking the box of spikenard on him ; "she hath wrought a good work on me". But after feeding the multitudes He would say, "Gather up the fragments that remain, that nothing be lost".

This was observing the divine rule, "There is a time to keep, and a time to cast away". If the prodigal service of the heart or hand in worship be no waste, the very crumbs of human food are sacred, and must not be cast away. He who vindicated the spending of 300 pence on one of these occasions, on the other would not let the fragments of three loaves be left on the ground. In His eyes such fragments were sacred. They were the food of life, the herb of the field, which God had given to man for his life. And life is a sacred thing. God is the God of the living. "To you it shall be for meat", God has said of it, and therefore Jesus would hallow it. "The tree of the field is man's life", the law had said, and accordingly had thus prescribed to them that were under the law—"When thou shalt besiege a city a long time, in making war against it to take it, thou shalt not destroy the trees thereof by forcing an axe against them : for thou mayest eat of them, and thou shalt not cut them down to employ them in the siege : only the trees that thou knowest are not trees for meat, thou shalt destroy and cut them down". (Deut. 20). It would have been waste, it would have been profaneness, to have thus abused the food of life, which was God's gift ; and Jesus in like purity, in the perfectness of God's living ordinance, would not let the fragments lie on the ground. "Gather up the fragments that remain," He said, "that nothing be lost".

These are but small incidents ; but all the circumstances of human life, as He passes through them, change as they may, or be they as minute as they may, are thus adorned by something of the moral glory that was ever brightening the path of His sacred, wearied feet. The eye of man was incapable of tracking it ; but to God it was all incense, a sacrifice of sweet savour, a sacrifice of rest, the meat offering of the sanctuary.

But again. The Lord did not judge of persons in relation to Himself,—a common fault with us all. We naturally judge of others according as they treat ourselves, and we make our interest in them the measure of their character and worth. But this was not the Lord. God is a God of knowledge, and by Him actions are weighed. He understands every action *fully*. In all its moral meaning He understands it, and according to that He weighs

it. And, as the image of the God of knowledge, we see our Lord Jesus Christ in the days of His ministry here, again and again. I may refer to Luke 11. There was the air of courtesy and good feeling towards Him in the Pharisee that invited Him to dine. But the Lord was "the God of knowledge", and as such He weighed this action in its full moral character.

The honey of courtesy, which is the best ingredient in social life in this world, should not pervert His taste or judgment. He approved things that are excellent. The civility which invited Him to dinner was not to determine the judgment of Him who carried the weights and measures of the sanctuary of God. It is the God of knowledge that this civility has on this occasion to confront, and it does not stand, it will not do. O how the tracing of this may rebuke us! The invitation covered a purpose. As soon as the Lord entered the house, the host acts the Pharisee, and not the host. He marvels that his guest had not washed before dinner. And the character he thus assumes at the beginning shows itself in full force at the end. And the Lord deals with the whole scene accordingly; for He weighed it as the God of knowledge. Some may say, that the courtesy He had received might have kept Him silent. But He could not look on this man simply as in relation to Himself. He was not to be *flattered* out of a just judgment. He exposes and rebukes, and the end of the scene justifies Him. "And as he said these things unto them, the scribes and Pharisees began to urge him vehemently, and to provoke him to speak of many things, laying wait for him, and seeking to catch something out of his mouth, that they might accuse him".

Very different, however, was His way in the house of another Pharisee, who in like manner had asked Him to dine. (See Luke 7). For Simon had no covered purpose in the invitation. Quite otherwise. He seemed to act the Pharisee too, silently accusing the poor sinner of the city, and his guest for admitting her approach. But appearances are not the ground of righteous judgments. Often the very same words, on different lips, have a very different mind in them. And therefore the Lord, the perfect weighmaster according to God, though He may rebuke Simon, and expose him to himself, knows him by name, and leaves his house as a guest should leave it. He distinguishes the Pharisee of Luke 7 from the Pharisee of Luke 11, though He dined with both of them. So we may look at the Lord with Peter in Matthew 16. Peter expresses fond and considerate attachment to his Master : "This be far from thee, Lord, this shall not be unto thee". But Jesus judged Peter's words only in their *moral* place. Hard indeed we find it to do this when we are personally gratified. "Get thee behind me, Satan", was not the answer which a merely amiable nature would have suggested to such words. But again, I say, our Lord did not listen to Peter's words simply as they expressed personal kindness and goodwill to Himself. He *judged* them, He weighed them, as in the presence of God, and at once found that the enemy had moved them ; for he that can transform himself into an angel of light is very often lurking in words of courtesy and kindness. And in the same way the Lord dealt with Thomas in John 20. Thomas had just worshipped Him. "My Lord and my God", he had said. But Jesus was not to be drawn from the high moral elevation that He filled, and from whence He heard and saw everything, even by words like these. They were genuine words, words of a mind which, enlightened of God, had repented toward the risen Saviour, and, instead of doubting any longer, worshipped. But Thomas had stood out as long as he could. He had exceeded. They had all been unbelieving as to the resurrection, but he had insisted that he would be still in unbelief till sense and sight came to deliver him. All this had been his moral condition ; and Jesus has this before Him, and puts Thomas in his right moral place, as He had put Peter. "Thomas, because thou hast seen me, thou hast believed. Blessed are they that have not seen, and yet have believed." Our hearts in such cases as these would have been taken by surprise. They could not have kept their ground in the face of these assaults, which the good will of Peter and the worship of Thomas would have made upon them. But our perfect Master stood for God and His truth, and not for Himself. The ark of old was not to be flattered. Israel may honour it, and bring it down to the battle, telling it, as it were, that now in its presence all *must* be well with them. But this will not do for the God of Israel. Israel falls before the Philistines, though the ark be thus in the battle ; and Peter and Thomas shall be rebuked, though Jesus, still the God of Israel, be honoured by them.

Angels have their joy over the repentance of sinners. "There is joy in the presence of the angels of God over one sinner that repenteth." It is happy to have this secret of heaven disclosed to us, and to read one illustration of it after another, as we do in Luke 15.

But there is something beyond this. The joy there,

though in heaven, is *public*. It utters itself, and has companionship. Very proper that it should be so ; very proper that the whole house should share it, and find it a common joy. But there is something beyond this. There is the joy of the *divine bosom*, as well as this joy of heaven. John 4 : 27-32 gives it to us, as Luke 15 gives us the public joy in heaven. And this joy of the divine bosom, I need not say, is the deeper thing. It is full, silent, and personal. It askes not to be raised or sustained by others. "I have meat to eat that ye know not of", is the language of the heart of Christ, as He tasted this joy. The glory was filling the house, so that the ministers of the house must stand by for a time. The Shepherd had but just brought home the stray one of the flock, having laid it on His shoulders rejoicing, and as yet the joy was all His own. The household had not been called to rejoice with Him, when the woman left him a saved and happy sinner. Disciples felt the character of the moment. They would not trespass. The fat reserved for the altar, the richest portion of the feast, "the food of God", was spread, and the disciples were silent, and stood apart. This was a wondrous moment—not many like it. The deep, unuttered joy of the divine bosom is known here, as the public ecstatic joy of heaven is known in Luke 15.

But He that could be thus feasted was weary betimes, and hungry, and thirsting. This is seen in the same chapter, John 4 ; as again in Mark 4. But there is this difference in the two cases : He finds sleep for His relief and restoration in Mark 4. He is independent of it in John 4. And why was this ? In Mark 4 He had gone through a day of toil, and in the evening He was

weary, as nature will be after labour, "Man goeth forth
to his work and to his labour until the evening". (Ps. 104).
Sleep is then provided for him, to restore him to his
service when morning returns. Jesus proved all this. He
was asleep on the pillow in the boat. In John 4 He is
weary again, hungry and thirsty too. He sits at the well,
like a tired traveller, waiting till the disciples came from
the neighbouring village with food. But when they come,
they find Him feasted and rested, and that too without
food, or drink or sleep. His weariness had had another
refreshment than what sleep would have brought Him.
He had been made happy by fruit to His labour in the
soul of a poor sinner. The woman had been sent away in
the liberty of the salvation of God. But there had been
no woman of Samaria in Mark 4, and He has therefore
to use the pillow in His weariness.

But how true all this is to the sensibilities of our common
humanity! We all understand it. The Lord's heart was
merry, as I may say, in John 4 ; but there was nothing
to make it merry in Mark 4. And we are taught to know
(and our experience sets to its seal that the word is true)
"that a merry heart doeth good like medicine, but a broken
spirit drieth the bones". (Prov. 17 : 22). So that the
Master can say in the one case, "I have meat to eat that ye
know not of", while in the other, He will use the pillow
which care for His weariness had provided.

How perfect in all its sympathies was the humanity
the Son had assumed! Surely, indeed, it was the common
humanity, apart from sin.

'Touched with a sympathy within,
He knows our feeble frame '

But again. There is a temptation in the time of confusion to cast up all as hopeless and gone ; and to say, it is endless and needless to be still distinguishing. All is in disorder and apostasy ; why then attempt to distinguish ?

But this was not the Lord. He was *in* the confusion, but not *of* it, as He was in the world, but not of it, as we said before of Him. He met all sorts of people, in all sorts of conditions, heaps upon heaps, where all should have been compact together ; but He held His even, narrow, unsoiled and undistracted way through it all. The pretensions of the Pharisee, the worldliness of the Herodian, the philosophy of the Sadducee, the fickleness of the multitude, the attempts of adversaries, and the ignorance and infirmities of disciples, were moral materials which He had to meet and answer every day.

And then the condition of things, as well as the characters of persons, exercised him ; the coin of Caesar circulating in Immanuel's land ; partition-walls all but in ruins ; Jew and gentile, clean and unclean, confounded, save as religious arrogancy might still retain them after its own manner. But His one golden rule expressed the perfectness of His passage through all—"Render unto Caesar the things that are Caesar's, and unto God the things that are God's". The remnant in the day of captivity, a like day of confusion, carried themselves beautifully, distinguishing things that differed, and not hopelessly casting all up. Daniel would advise the king, but not eat his meat : Nehemiah would serve in the palace, but not suffer the Moabite or the Ammonite in the house of the Lord : Mordecai would guard the king's life, but would not bow to the Amalekite : Ezra and Zerubbabel would accept favours from the Persian, but not Samaritan help, nor gentile marriages : and the captives would pray for the peace of Babylon, but would not sing Zion's songs there. All this was beautiful ; and the Lord, in His day, was *perfect in this remnant-character*. And all this has a voice for us ; for ours is a day, in its character of confusion, not inferior to these days of the captives, or of Jesus. And we, like them, are not to act on the hopelessness of the scene, but know still how to render to Caesar the things that are Caesar's, and to God the things that are God's.

All His moral beauty becomes a pattern to us. But then we see Him stand in God's relationship to evil also, and that is a place which, of course, we never could fill. He touched the leper, and He touched the bier, and yet He was undefiled. He had God's relationship to sin. He knew good and evil, but was in divine supremacy over it ; knowing such things as God knows them. Had He been other than He was, these touches of the bier and of the leper would have defiled Him. He must have been put outside the camp, and gone through the cleansing which the law prescribed. But nothing of this kind do we see in Him. He was not an unclean Jew ; He was not merely undefiled, He was undefilable; and yet, such was the mystery of His person, such the perfection of the manhood in company with the Godhead in Him, that the temptation was as real in Him as was the undefilableness.

But we pause. Our place towards much of this needed, though mysterious and deeply precious truth, is to receive it and worship, rather than to discuss and analyse it*. It

---

* His death, I may here take occasion to say, was the perfecting of His moral glory. of which I speak, (Phil. 2.) Of course, I know it was a great deal more than that also. But, among other things, it was that.

is happy, however, to one's own spirit, to mark the yearnings of some simple souls, who give you the impression that it is *Himself* that is before them. We ofttimes traffic with truths in such wise as in the end leaves with us a rebuking conviction that we did not reach Himself, though so occupied. We find out that we had been loitering in the avenue.

The Lord was "poor, yet making rich",—"having nothing, and yet possessing all things". These high and wondrous conditions were exhibited in Him, in ways that were and must have been peculiar—altogether His own. He would receive ministry from some godly women out of their substance, and yet minister to the need of all around Him out of the treasures of the fulness of the earth. He would feed thousands in desert places, and yet be Himself an hungered, waiting for the return of His disciples with victuals from a neighbouring village. This is "having nothing, and yet possessing all things". But while thus poor, both needy and exposed, *nothing that in the least savoured of meanness* is ever seen attaching to His condition. He never begs, though He have not a penny ; for when He wanted to see one (not to use it for Himself) He had to ask to be shown it. He never runs away, though exposed, and His life jeoparded, as we speak, in the place where He was. He withdraws Himself, or passes by as hidden. And thus, again, I may say, nothing mean, nothing unbecoming full personal dignity attaches to Him, though poverty and exposure were His lot every day.

Blessed and beautiful! Who could preserve under our eye such an Object, so perfect, so unblemished, so exquisitely, delicately pure, in all the minute and most

ordinary details of human life! Paul does not give us this.
None could give it to us but Jesus, the God-man. The
peculiarities of His virtues in the midst of the ordinariness
of His circumstances tell us of His Person. It must be a
peculiar Person, it must be the divine Man, if I may so
express Him, that could give us such peculiarities in such
common-place conditions. Paul does not give us anything
like it, again I say. There was great dignity and moral
elevation about him, I know. If any one may be received
as exhibiting that, let us agree that it was he. But his
path is not that of Jesus ; he is in danger of his life, and
he uses his nephew to protect him. Again, his friends
let him down the wall of the town in a basket. I do not
say he begs or asks for it, but he acknowledges money
sent to him. I say not how Paul avowed himself a Pharisee
in the mixed assembly, in order to shelter himself ; or how
he spake evil of the High Priest that was judging him.
Such conduct was morally wrong ; and I am speaking
here only of such cases as were, though not morally wrong,
below the full personal and moral dignity that marks the
way of Christ. Nor is the flight into Egypt, as it is called,
an exception in this characteristic of the Lord ; for that
journey was taken to fulfil prophecy, and under the
authority of a divine oracle.

But all this is really, not only moral glory, but it is a
moral wonder—marvellous how the pen that was held
by a human hand could ever have delineated such beauties.
We are to account for it, as has been observed before and
by others, only by its being a truth, a living reality. We
are shut up to that blessed necessity. Still further, as we go
on with this blessed truth, it is written, "Let your speech

be always with grace, seasoned with salt, that ye may know how ye ought to answer every man". Our words should prove themselves as thus, always with grace, by ministering good to others, "grace to the hearers". This, however, will often be in the pungency of admonition or rebuke ; and at times with decision or severity, even with indignation and zeal ; and thus they will be "seasoned with salt", as the scripture speaks. And having these fine qualities, being gracious and yet salted, they will bear witness that we know how to answer every man.

Among all other forms of it, the Lord Jesus illustrated this form of moral perfectness. He knew how to answer every man, as with words which were always to his soul's profit, whether men would hear, or whether they would forbear ; but at times seasoned, nay, seasoned highly with salt.

Thus, in answering inquiries, He did not so much purpose to satisfy *them*, as to reach the *conscience or the condition of the inquirer*.

In His silence, or refusal to answer at all, when He stood before the Jew or the gentile at the end, before either the priests, or Pilate, or Herod, we can trace the same perfect fitness as we do in His words or answers ; witnessing to God, that at least One among the sons of men knew "a time to keep silence, and a time to speak".

Great variety in His very tone and manner also presents itself in all this ; and all this variety, minute as it was as well as great, was part of this fragrance before God. Sometimes His word was gentle, sometimes peremptory ; sometimes He reasons ; sometimes He rebukes at once ;

and sometimes conducts calm reasoning up to the heated point of solemn condemnation ; for it is the *moral* of the occasion He always weighs.

Matthew 15 has struck me as a chapter in which this perfection, in much of its various beauty and excellency, may be seen. In the course of it the Lord is called to answer the Pharisees, the multitude, the poor afflicted stranger from the coasts of Tyre, and His own disciples, again and again, in their different exposure of either their stupidity or their selfishness , and we may notice His different style of rebuke and of reasoning, of calm, patient teaching, and of faithful, wise, and gracious training of the soul : and we cannot but feel how fitting all this variety was to the place or occasion that called it forth. And such was the beauty and the fitness of His neither *teaching* nor *learning*, in Luke 2, but only hearing and asking questions. To have *taught* then would not have been in season, a child as He was in the midst of His elders. To have learnt would not have been in full fidelity to the light, the eminent and bright light, which He knew He carried in Himself ; for we may surely say of Him, "He was wiser than the ancients, and had more understanding than his teachers". I do not mean as God, but as One "filled with wisdom", as was then said of Him. But He knew in the perfection of grace how to use this fulness of wisdom, and He is, therefore, not presented to us by the evangelist in the midst of the doctors in the temple, at the age of twelve, either *teaching* or *learning* ; but it is simply said of Him, that He was hearing and asking questions. Strong in spirit, filled with wisdom, and the grace of God upon Him, is the description of Him then, as He grew up in tender years ; and when a

Man, conversing in the world, His speech was always with grace, seasoned with salt, as of One who knew how to answer every man. What perfection and beauty suited to the different seasons of childhood and manhood!

And further. We find Him, besides this, also in various other conditions. At times He is *slighted and scorned*, watched and hated by adversaries, retiring, as it were, to save His life from their attempts and purposes. At times He is *weak*, followed only by the poorest of the people ; wearied, too, and hungry and athirst, debtor to the service of some loving women, who felt as though they owed Him everything. At times He is *compassionating the multitude* in all gentleness, or companying with His disciples in their repasts or in their journeying, conversing with them as a man would with his friends. At times He is *in strength and honour* before us, doing wonders, letting out some rays of glory ; and though in His person and circumstances nothing and nobody in the world, a carpenter's son, without learning or fortune, yet making a greater stir among men, and that, too, at times in the thoughts of the ruling ones on earth, than man ever made.

Childhood, and manhood, and human life in all its variousness, thus gives Him to us. Would that the heart could hold Him! There is a perfection in some of the minute features that tell of the divine hand that was delineating them. Awkward work would any penman, unkept, unguided by the Spirit, have made of certain occasions where these strokes and touches are seen. As when the Lord wanted to comment on the current money of the land, He asked to be shewn it, and does not find it about Himself. Indeed, we may be sure He carried none of it. Thus, the moral beauties of the action flowed from the moral perfection of His condition within.

He asked His disciples, in the hour of Gethsemane, to *watch with Him* ; but He did not ask them to *pray for Him*. He would claim sympathy. He prized it in the hour of weakness and pressure, and would have the hearts of His companions bound to Him then. Such a desire was of the moral glory that formed the human perfection that was in Him ; but while He felt this and did this, He could not ask them to stand as in the divine presence on His behalf. He would have them give themselves to Him, but He could not seek them to give themselves to God for Him. Thus, He asked them again, I say, to watch with Him, but He did not ask them to pray for Him. When shortly or immediately afterwards He linked praying and watching together, it was of themselves and for themselves He spoke, saying, "Watch and pray, that ye enter not into temptation". Paul could say to his fellow-saints, "Ye also helping together by prayer to God for us : pray for us, for we trust we have a good conscience". But such was not the language of Jesus. I need not say, it could not have been ; but the pen that writes for us such a life, and delineates for us such a character, is held by the Spirit of God. None other than the Spirit could write thus.

He did good, and lent, hoping for nothing again. He gave, and His left hand did not know what His right hand was doing. Never in one single instance, as I believe, did He claim either the person or the service of those whom He restored and delivered. He never made the deliverance He wrought a title to service. Jesus loved, and healed, and saved, looking for nothing again. He would not let

Legion, the Gadarene, be with Him. The child at the foot
of the mount He delivered back to his father. The daughter
of Jairus He left in the bosom of her family. The widow's
son at Nain He restores to his mother. He claims none of
them. Does Christ give, in order that He may receive
again ? Does He not (perfect Master!) illustrate His own
principle—"Do good, and lend, hoping for nothing again" ?
The nature of grace is to impart to others, not to enrich
itself : and He came, that in Him and His ways it might
shine in all the exceeding riches and glory that belong to it.
He found servants in this world ; but He did not first heal
them, and then claim them. He called them, and endowed
them. They were the fruit of the energy of His Spirit, and
of affections kindled in hearts constrained by His love.
And sending them forth, He said to them, "Freely ye have
received, freely give". Surely there is something beyond
human conception in the delineation of such a character.
One repeats that thought again and again. And very
happy it is to add, that it is in the very simplest forms this
moral glory of the Lord shines forth at times—such forms
as are at once intelligible to all the perceptions and sympathies of the heart. Thus He never refused the feeblest
faith, though He accepted and answered, and that too with
delight, the approaches and demands of the boldest.

The strong faith, which drew upon Him without ceremony or apology, in full, immediate assurance, was ever
welcome to Him ; while the timid soul, that approached
Him as one that was ashamed and would excuse itself,
was encouraged and blessed. His lips at once bore away
from the heart of the poor leper the one only thing that
hung over that heart as a cloud. "Lord, if thou wilt,

thou canst make me clean", said he. "I will ; be thou clean", said Jesus. But immediately afterwards the same lips uttered the fulness of the heart, when the clear, unquestioning faith of the gentile centurion was witnessed, and when the bold, earnest faith of a family in Israel broke up the roof of the house where He was, that they might let down their sick one before him.

When a weak faith appealed to the Lord, He granted the blessing it sought, but He rebuked the seeker. But even this rebuke is full of comfort to us ; for it seems to say, "Why did you not make freer, fuller, happier use of Me ?" Did we value the giver, as we do the gift,—the heart of Christ as well as His hand, this *rebuke* of weak faith would be just as welcome as the *answer* to it.

And if little faith be thus reproved, strong faith must be grateful. And therefore we have reason to know what a fine sight was under the eye of the Lord, when, in that case already looked at, they broke up the roof of the house in order to reach Him. It was indeed, right sure I am, a grand spectacle for the eye of the divine and bounteous Jesus. *His heart* was entered by that action, as surely as *the house in Capernaum* was entered by it.

We see glories and humilities in our Redeemer : we do indeed ; for we need each.

The One who sat on the well in Sychar is He who now sits on high in heaven. He that ascended is He that descended. Dignities and condescensions are with Him;— a seat at the right hand of God, and yet a stooping to wash the feet of His saints here. What a combination! No abatement of His honours, though suiting Himself to our poverty : nothing wanting that can serve us, though glorious, and stainless, and complete in Himself.

Selfishness is wearied by trespass and importunity. "He will not rise because he is his friend ; but because of his importunity he will rise and give him as much as he needeth." Thus it is with man, or selfishness ; it is otherwise with God, or love ; for God, in Isaiah 7, is the contradiction of man in Luke 11.

It is the unbelief, that would not draw on Him, that refused to ask a blessing, and get it with a seal and a witness, that wearied God—not importunity, but, as I may say, the absence of it. And all this divine blessedness and excellency, which is thus seen in the Jehovah of the house of David in Isaiah 7 reappears in the Lord Jesus Christ of the evangelists, and in His different dealing with weak faith and full faith.

All these things that we are able to discover bespeak His perfections ; but how small a part of them do we reach!

We are aware in how many different ways our fellow-disciples try and tempt us, as, no doubt, we do them. We see, or we fancy we see, some bad quality in them, and we find it hard to go on in further company with them. And yet in all this, or in much of it, the fault may be with ourselves, mistaking a want of conformity of taste or judgment with ourselves, for something to be condemned in them.

But the Lord could not be thus mistaken ; and yet He was never "overcome of evil", but was ever "overcoming evil with good"—the evil that was in them with the good that was in Himself. Vanity, ill-temper, indifference about others, and carefulness about themselves, ignorance after painstaking to instruct, were of the things in them which He had to suffer continually. His walk with them, in its way and measure, was a day of provocation, as the forty years in the wilderness had been. Israel again tempted the Lord, I may say, but again proved Him. Blessed to tell it ; they *provoked* Him, but by this they *proved* Him. He suffered, but He took it patiently. He never gave them up. He warned and taught, rebuked and condemned them, but never gave them up. Nay ; at the end of their walk together, He is nearer to them than ever.

Perfect and excellent this is, and comforting to us. The Lord's dealing with the conscience never touches His heart. We lose nothing by His rebukes. And He who does not withdraw His heart from us when He is dealing with our conscience, is quick to restore our souls, that the conscience, so to express it, may be enabled soon to leave His school, and the heart find its happy freedom in His presence again. As expressed in that hymn, which some of us know—

> 'Still sweet 'tis to discover,
>   If clouds have dimm'd my sight,
> When pass'd, Eternal Lover,
>   Toward me, as e'er, thou'rt bright.'

And I would further notice, that in the characters which, in the course of His ministry, He is called to take up (it may be for only an occasion, or a passing moment), we see the same perfection, the same moral glory, as in the path He treads daily. As, for instance, that of a Judge, as in Matt. 23, and that of an Advocate or Pleader in Matt. 22. But I only suggest this : the theme is too abundant. Every step, word, and action, carries with it a ray of this glory ; and the eye of God had more to fill it in the life of Jesus, than it would have had in an eternity of Adam's innocency. It was in the midst of our moral ruin Jesus walked ; and from such a region as that He has sent up to the throne on high a richer sacrifice of sweet-smelling savour than Eden, and the Adam of Eden, had it continued unsoiled for ever, would or could have rendered. *Time made no change in the Lord.* Kindred instances of grace and character in Him, before and after His resurrection, give us possession of this truth, which is of such importance to us. We know what He is this moment, and what He will be for ever from what He has already been—in character as in nature—in relationship to us, as well as in Himself—"the same yesterday, today, and for ever". The very mention of this is blessed. Sometimes we may be grieved at changes, sometimes we may desire them. In different ways we all prove the fickle, uncertain nature of that which constitutes human life. Not only circumstances, which are changeful to a proverb, but associations, friendships, affections, characters, continually undergo variations which surprise and sadden us. We are hurried from stage to stage of life ; but unchilled affections and unsullied principles are rarely borne along with us, either in ourselves or our companions. But Jesus was the same after His resurrection as He had been before, though late events had put Him and His disciples at a greater distance than companions had ever known, or could ever know. *They* had betrayed their unfaithful hearts, forsaking Him and fleeing in the hour of His weakness and need ; while *He* for their sakes had gone through death—such a death as never could have been borne by another, as would have crushed the creature itself. They were still but poor feeble Galileans,—He was glorified with all power in heaven and on earth.

But these things worked no change ; " nor height, nor depth, nor any other creature", as the apostle speaks, could do that. Love defies them all, and He returns to them the Jesus whom they had known before. He is their companion in labour after His resurrection, nay, after His ascension, as He had been in the days of His ministry and sojourn with them. This we learn in the last verse of Mark. On the sea, in the day of Matt. 14, they thought that they saw a spirit, and cried out for fear ; but the Lord gave them to know that it was He Himself that was there, near to them, and in grace, though in divine strength and sovereignty over nature. And so in Luke 24, or after He was risen, He takes the honey-comb and the fish, and eats before them, that with like certainty and ease of heart they might know that it was He Himself. And He would have them handle Him, and see ; telling them, that a spirit had not flesh and bones, as they might then prove that He had.

In John 3 He led a slow-hearted Rabbi into the light and way of truth, bearing with him in all patient grace. And thus did He again in Luke 24, after that He was risen, with the two slow-hearted ones who were finding their way home to Emmaüs.

In Mark 4 He allayed the fears of His people ere He rebuked their unbelief. He said to the winds and the waves, "Peace, be still", before He said to the disciples, "How is it that ye have no faith ?" And thus did He, as the risen One, in John xxi. He sits and dines with Peter, in full and free fellowship, as without a breach in the Spirit, ere

He challenges him and awakens his conscience by the words, "Simon, son of Jonas, lovest thou me?"

The risen Jesus who appeared to Mary Magdalene, the evangelist takes care to tell us, was He who in other days had cast seven devils out of her—and she herself knew the voice that then called her by her name, as a voice that her ear had long been familiar with. What identity between the humbled and the glorified One, the healer of sinners and the Lord of the world to come! How all tell us, that in character as in divine personal glory, He that descended is the same also that ascended. John, too, in company with his risen Lord, is recognized as the one who had leaned on His bosom at the supper. "I am Jesus", was the answer from the ascended place, the very highest place in heaven, the right hand of the throne of the majesty there, when Saul of Tarsus demanded, "Who art thou, Lord?" (Acts 9). And all this is so individual and personal in its application to us. It is our own very selves that are interested in this. Peter, for himself, knows his Master, the same to him before and after the resurrection. In Matt. 16 the Lord rebukes him ; but shortly after takes him up to the hill with Him, with as full freedom of heart as if nothing had happened. And so with the same Peter,— in John 21 he is again rebuked. He had been busy, as was his way, meddling with what was beyond him. "Lord, what shall this man do?" says he, looking at John,—and his Master has again to rebuke him—"What is that to thee?" But again, as in the face of this rebuke, sharp and peremptory as it was, the Lord immediately afterwards has him, together with John, in His train, or in His company up to heaven. It was a *rebuked* Peter who had once gone with the Lord to the holy mount ; and it is a *rebuked* Peter, the same rebuked Peter, who now goes with the Lord to heaven ; or, if we please, to the hill of glory, the mount of transfiguration, a second time.*

Full indeed of strong consolation is all this. This is Jesus our Lord, the same yesterday, today, and for ever ; the same in the day of His ministry, after His resurrection, now in the ascended heavens, and so for ever ; and as He sustains the same character, and approves Himself by the same grace after as before the resurrection, so does He redeem all His pledges left with His disciples.

Whether it be on His own lips, or on the lips of His angels, it is still now as then, since He rose as before He suffered, "Fear not" : He had spoken to His disciples before of giving them *His* peace ; and we find He does this afterwards in the most emphatic manner. He pronounces peace upon them in the day of John 20 ; and having done so, shows them His hands and His side ; where, as in symbolic language, they might read their title to a peace wrought out and purchased for them by Himself, His peace, entirely His own, as procured only by Himself, and now theirs by indefeasible, unchangeable title.

In earlier days the Lord said to them, "Because I live, ye shall live also" ; and now in risen days, in the days of the risen Man, in possession of victorious life, He imparts that life to them in the most full and perfect measure of it, breathing on them, and saying, "Receive ye the Holy Spirit".

* Some seem to judge that it was deep love in Peter to John, that led him to ask the Lord about him. I deny that.

The world was not to see Him again, as He had also said to them ; but they were to see Him. And so it comes to pass. He was seen of them for forty days and He spake to them of the things pertaining to the kingdom of God. But this was all in secret : the world has not seen Him since the hour of Calvary, nor will they till they see Him in judgment.

As a humbler, lowlier witness of His full fidelity to all His pledges, we may observe, He meets His people in Galilee, as He had promised them. As a larger expression of the same, I may also observe, He takes them to the Father in heaven, as He had also promised them, sending a message to them, that He was ascending to *His* Father and to *their* Father, to *His* God and to *their* God. And thus, whether it was in our Galilee on earth, or in His own home in heaven, that His presence had been pledged to them, both are alike made good to them. And well may we meditate on the condescendings, the faithfulness, the fulness, the simplicity, the greatness, the elevation, of all that forms and marks His path before us. The Lord had very much to do with Peter, beyond any of the disciples while He was ministering in the midst of them, and we find it the same after He rose from the dead. Peter is the one to occupy, as I may say, the whole of the last chapter in John. There the Lord carries on with him the gracious work he had begun ere He left him, and carried it on exactly from the point where He had left it. Peter had betrayed special self-confidence. Though all should be offended, yet would not he, he said ; and though he should die with his Master, he would not deny Him. But his Master had told him of the vanity of such boasts and had told him also of His prayer for him, so that his faith should not fail. And when the boast was found to have been indeed a vanity, and Peter denied his Lord, even with an oath, his Lord looked on him, and this look had its blessed operation. The prayer and the look had availed. The prayer had kept his faith from failing, but the look had broken his heart. Peter did not "go away", but Peter wept, and "wept bitterly". At the opening of this chapter, we find Peter in this condition—in the condition in which the prayer and the look had put him. That his faith had not failed, he is enabled to give very sweet proof ; for as soon as he learns that it was his Lord who was on the shore, he threw himself into the water to reach Him ; not, however, as a penitent, as though he had not already wept, but as one that could trust himself to His presence in full assurance of heart ; and in that character his most blessed and gracious Lord accepts him, and they dine together on the shore. The prayer and the look had thus already done their work with Peter, and they are not to be repeated. The Lord simply goes on with His work thus begun, to conduct it to its perfection. Accordingly, the *prayer* and the *look* are now followed by *the word*. Restoration follows conviction and tears. Peter is put into the place of strengthening his brethren, as his Lord had once said to him ; and also into the place of glorifying God by his death, a privilege he had forfeited by his unbelief and denial.

This was the word of restoration, following the prayer which had already sustained Peter's faith, and the look which had already broken his heart. He had in the day of John 13 taught this same loved Peter, that a washed man need not be washed again, save only his feet ; and exactly in this way He now deals with him. He does not put him again through the process of Luke 5, when the draught of fishes overwhelmed him, and he found out that he was a sinner ; but He does wash his soiled feet. He restores him, and puts Himself in His due place again. (See John 21 15-17.)

Perfect Master! the same to us yesterday, today and for ever ; the same in gracious, perfect skill of love, going on with the work He had already begun, resuming, as the risen Lord, the service which He had left unfinished when He was taken from them, resuming it at the very point, knitting the past to the present service in the fullest grace and skill!

And a little further still, as to His redeeming His pledges and promises. There was a very distinguished one which He gave them after He had risen. I mean, what He calls "the promise of the Father", and "power from on high". This promise was made to them in the day of Luke 24, after He had risen, and it was fulfilled to them in the day of Acts 2, after He had ascended, and was glorified.

Surely this only continues the story and the testimony of His faithfulness. All witness for Him,—His life ere He suffered, His resurrection intercourses with His disciples, and now what He has done since He ascended, —that no variableness neither shadow of turning is found in Him.

And I would not pass another instance of this, which we get again in Luke 24. The risen Lord there recognizes the very place in which He had left His disciples in His earlier instructions. "These are the words", says He, "which I spake unto you when I was yet with you, that all things must be fulfilled, which were written in the law of Moses, and in the prophets, and in the psalms, concerning me". He thus reminds them that He had already told them, that Scripture was the great witness of the divine mind, that all found *written there* must surely be *accomplished here.* And now what does He do? That which is the simple, consistent following out of this His previous teaching. "Then opened he their understanding, that they might understand the Scriptures." His *power* now knits itself with His *instructions* before. He is making good in them what He had already communicated to them.*

But even further, in some sense, the very style and spirit of this intercourse with His disciples during that interval of forty days is still the same. He knows them then *by name,* as He had before. He manifests Himself to them *by the same methods.* He was the host at the table, though bidden there only as a guest, a second time, or after, as before, His resurrection (John 2 ; Luke 24) ; and in the deep sense and apprehension of their souls they treat His presence as the same. On returning to Him at the well of Sychar in John 4, they would not intrude, but tread softly. And so on their reaching Him after the draught of fishes, in John 21, they tread softly again, judging a second time from the character of the moment, that their words must be few, though their hearts were filled with wonder and joy.

What links, tender and yet strong, are thus formed between Him who has been already known to us in the

* To our comfort I may add, that after He had risen, He never once reminded His disciples of their late desertion of Him in the hour of His sorrow.

daily walks of human life, and Him who is to be known to us for ever! He came down first into our circumstances, and then He takes us into His. But in ours we have learnt Him, and *learnt Him for ever*. This is a very happy truth. Peter witnesses it to us. I have looked at this scene already with another intent. I must now give it a second look.

At the draught of fishes in Luke 5, or before the resurrection, Peter was convicted. The *fisherman* Peter, in his own eyes, became the *sinner* Peter. "Depart from me, for I am a sinful man, O Lord." The draught of fishes (giving proof that the stranger who had asked for the loan of his boat was the Lord of the fulness of the sea) had brought Peter, in spirit, into the presence of God, and there he learnt himself. We never, indeed, learn that lesson anywhere else. But the Lord at that moment, as from the glory, spoke comfortably to him. He had said, "Fear not", and Peter was at ease. The glory or the presence of God had now a home for him as well as conviction, and Peter is in full quietness of heart before the Lord. And accordingly, at the second draught of fishes, in John 21, after the resurrection, Peter was still at ease, and had only to practise the lesson which he had already learnt. And he does so. He experiences the presence of the Lord of glory to be a home for him. He proves in himself, and witnesses to us, that *what he had learnt of Jesus he had learnt for ever*. He did not know the Stranger on the shore to be Jesus ; but when John revealed that fact to him, the Stranger was a stranger to him no more, but the sooner and the nearer he could get to Him the better.

What further consolation is this! if it be joy to know that He is the same, whether here or there, —whether in our world or in His own world, —in our ruined circumstances, or in His own glorious circumstances,—what further joy is it to see one of ourselves, as Peter was, experiencing the blessedness of such a fact in his own spirit!

Jesus—the same, indeed—faithful and true! All the pledges He had given them ere He suffered, He makes good after He rose : all the characters He had sustained in the midst of them then, He sustains now.

The Lord was continually *giving*, but He was rarely assenting. He made great *communications* where He found but little communion. This magnifies or illustrates His goodness. There was, as it were, nothing to draw Him forth, and yet He was ever imparting. He was as the Father in heaven, of whom He Himself spoke, making His sun rise on the evil and on the good, and sending His rain on the just and the unjust. This tells us what He is, to His praise—what we are, to our shame.

But He was not only thus, as the Father in heaven, the reflection of such a One in His doings, but He was also in this world as "the unknown God", as Paul speaks. The darkness did not comprehend Him ; the world, neither by its religion nor its wisdom, knew Him. The rich aboundings of His grace, the purity of His kingdom, the foundation and title upon which the glory He sought in such a world as this alone could rest, were all strangers to the thoughts of the children of men. All this is seen in the deep moral mistakes they were continually making. When, for instance, the multitude were exceedingly hailing the King and the kingdom in His person, in Luke 19, "Master, rebuke thy disciples", the Pharisees say. They would not brook the thought of the throne belonging to such a One. It was presumption in Him, Jesus of Nazareth as He was, to allow the royal joy to surround Him. They knew not—they had not learnt—the secret of true honour in this false, fallen world of ours. They had not learnt the mystery of "a root out of a dry ground", nor had they in spirit perceived "the arm of the Lord". (Isa. 53.) It was where His own Spirit led, that discoveries were made of Him, and such are very sweet, and various, too, in their measure.

In Mark 1 His ministry, in its grace and power, is used by many. People under all kinds of diseases come to Him, congregations listen to Him, and own the authority with which He spake. A leper brings his leprosy to Him, thereby apprehending Him as the God of Israel. In different measures, there was then some knowledge of Him, either who He was, or what He had ; but when we enter chapter 2, we get knowledge of Him expressing itself in a brighter, richer way : we get samples of the faith that *understood* Him ; and this is the deeper thing.

The company at Capernaum, who bring their palsied friend to Him, understand Him, as well as use Him ; understand Him, I mean, in Himself, in His character, in the habits and tastes of His mind. The very style in which they reach Him to get at Him tells us this. It was not *approaching* as though they were reserved, and doubtful, and overawed. It was more : "I will not let thee go, except thou bless me"—a thing more welcome to Him, more according to the way that *love* would have us take. They ask no leave, they use no ceremony, but they break up the roof of the house, that they may reach Him ; all this telling us that they *knew* Him as well as *used* Him ; knew that He delighted in having His grace trusted and His power used by our necessities without reserve. So Levi, shortly afterwards, in the same chapter. He makes a feast, and seats publicans and others at it, in company with Jesus. And this, in like manner, tells us that Levi *knew* Him. He knew whom he *entertained*, as Paul tells us he knew whom he *believed*.

This knowledge of the Lord is truly blessed! It is divine! Flesh and blood does not give it, His kinsfolk had it not. They said of Him, when He was spending Himself in service, "He is beside himself". But faith makes great discoveries of Him, and acts upon such discoveries. It may seem to carry us beyond due bounds at times, beyond the things that are orderly and well measured ; but in God's esteem it never does. The multitude tell Bartimeus to hold his peace, but he will not ; for he knows Jesus as Levi knows Him.

It is His full work that we are not prepared for, and yet therein is its glory. He meets us in all our need, but, at the same time, He brings God in. He healed the sick, but He preached the kingdom also. This, however, did not suit man. Strange this may appear, for man knows full well how to value his own advantages. He knows the joy of the restored nature. But such is the enmity of the carnal mind against God, that if blessing come in company with the presence of God, it will not receive a welcome. And from Christ it could not come in any other way. He will glorify God as well as relieve the sinner. God has been dishonoured in this world, as man has been ruined in it—self-ruined ; and the Lord, the repairer of the breach, is doing a perfect work—vindicating the name and truth of God, declaring His kingdom and its rights, and manifesting His glory, just as much as He is redeeming and quickening the lost, dead sinner.

This will not do for man. He would be well taken care of himself, and let the glory of God fare as it may. Such is man. But when, through faith, any poor sinner is otherwise minded, and can indeed rejoice in the glory of God, very beautiful is the sight. And we see such a one in the Syro-Phoenician. The glory of the ministry of Christ addressed itself to her soul brightly and powerfully. Apparently, in spite of her grief, the Lord Jesus asserts God's principles, and, as a stranger, He passes her by. "I am not sent", He says, "but to the lost sheep of the house of Israel . . . It is not meet to take the children's bread, and to cast it unto the dogs". But she bows, she owns the Lord as the steward of the truth of God, and would not for a moment suppose that He would surrender that trust (the truth and principles of God) to her and her necessities. She would have God be glorified according to His own counsels, and Jesus continue the faithful Witness of those counsels, and the Servant of the divine good pleasure, be it to herself as it may. "Truth, Lord", she answers, vindicating all that He had said ; but, in full consistency with it, she adds, "yet the dogs under the table eat of the children's crumbs".

All this is lovely—the fruit of divine light in her soul. The mother in Luke 2 is quite below this gentile woman in Mark 7. She did not know that Jesus was to be about His Father's business, but this stranger knew that that was the very business He was always to be about. She would let God's way, in the faithful hand of Christ, be exalted, though she herself were thereby set aside, even in her sorrows.

This was knowledge of Him indeed ; this was accepting Him in his *full* work, as One who stood for God in a world that had rebelled against Him, as well as for the poor worthless sinner that had destroyed himself.

It is not well to be always understood. Our ways and habits should be those of strangers, citizens of a foreign country, whose language and laws, and customs are but poorly known here. Flesh and blood cannot appreciate them, and therefore it is not well with the saints of God when the world understands them.

His kinsfolk were ignorant of Jesus. Did the mother know Him when she wanted Him to display His power, and provide wine for the feast ? Did His brethren know Him when they said to Him, "If thou do these things, show thyself to the world". What a thought! an endeavour to lead the Lord Jesus to make Himself, as we say, "a man of the world!" Could there have been *knowledge of Him* in the hearts which indited such a thought as that ? Most distant, indeed, from such knowledge they were, and therefore it is immediately added by the evangelist, "for neither did his brethren believe in him". (John 7). They understood His *power*, but not His *principles* ; for, after the manner of men, they connect the possession of power or talents with the serving of a man's interest in the world.

But Jesus was the contradiction of this, as I need not say ; and the worldly-minded kindred in the flesh could not understand Him. His principles were foreign to such a world. They were despised, as was David's dancing before the ark in the thoughts of a daughter of king Saul.

But what attractiveness there would have been in Him for any eye or heart that had been opened by the Spirit! This is witnessed to us by the apostles. They knew but little about Him *doctrinally*, and they got nothing by remaining with Him— I mean nothing in this world. Their condition in the world was anything but improved by their walking with Him ; and it cannot be said that they availed themselves of His miraculous power. Indeed, they questioned it rather than used it. And yet they clung to Him. They did not company with Him, because they eyed Him as the full and ready storehouse of all provisions for them. On no one occasion, I believe we may say, did they use the power that was in Him for themselves. And yet, there they were with Him,—troubled when He talked of leaving, and found weeping when they thought they had indeed lost Him.

Surely, we may again say, What attractiveness there must have been in Him, for any eye or heart that had been opened by the Spirit, or drawn by the Father! And with what authority one look or one word from Him would enter at times! We see this in Matthew. That one word on the Lord's lips, "Follow me!" was enough. And this authority and this attractiveness was felt by men of the most opposite temperaments. The slow-hearted, reasoning Thomas, and the ardent, uncalculating Peter, were alike kept near and around this wondrous Centre. Even Thomas would breathe in that presence the spirit of the earnest

Peter, and say under force of this attraction, "Let us also go, that we may die with him".

Shall we not say, What will it be to see and feel all this by and by in its perfection! when all, gathered from every clime, and colour, and character, of the wide-spread human family—all nations, kindreds, people, and tongues, are with Him and around Him in a world worthy of Him! We may dwell, in memory, on these samples of His preciousness to hearts like our own, and welcome them as pledges of that which, in hope, is ours as well as theirs.

The light of God shines at times before us, leaving us, as we may have power, to discern it, to enjoy it, to use it, to follow it. It does not so much challenge us or exact of us ; but, as I said, it shines before us, that we may reflect it, if we have grace. We see it doing its work after this manner in the early church at Jerusalem. The light of God there *exacted* nothing. It shone brightly and power-fully ; but that was all. Peter spoke the language of that light, when he said to Ananias, "While it remained, was it not thine own? and after it was sold, was it not in thy power?" It had made no demands upon Ananias, it simply shone in its beauty beside him or before him, that he might walk in it according to his measure. And such, in a great sense, is the moral glory of the Lord Jesus. Our first duty to that light is to learn from it *what He is*. We are not to begin by anxiously and painfully measuring ourselves by it, but by calmly, and happily, and thankfully learning Him in all His perfect moral humanity. And surely this glory is departed! There is no living image of it here. We have its *record* in the evangelists, but not its *reflection* anywhere.

But having its record, we may say, as one of our own poets has said,

> 'There has one object been disclosed on earth
> That might commend the place : but now 'tis gone :
> Jesus is with the Father'.

But though not here, beloved, He is just what He was. We are to know Him as it were by *memory* ; and memory has no capacity to weave fictions ; memory can only turn over living truthful pages. And thus we know Him for His own eternity. In an eminent sense, the disciples knew Him *personally*. It was His person, His presence, Himself, that was their attraction. And if one may speak for others, it is more of this we need. We may be busy in acquainting ourselves with truths about Him, and we may make proficiency that way ; but with all our knowledge, and with all the disciples' ignorance, they may leave us far behind in the power of a commanding affection towards Himself. And surely, beloved, we will not refuse to say, that it is well when the heart is drawn by Him beyond what the knowledge we have of Him may account for. It tells us that He Himself has been rightly apprehended. And there are simple souls still that exhibit this ; but generally it is not so. Now-a-days, our light, our acquaintance with truth, is beyond the measure of the answer of our heart to Himself. And it is painful to us, if we have any just sensibilities at all, to discover this.

'The prerogative of our christian faith', says one, 'the secret of its strength is this, that all which it has, and all which it offers, is laid up in a *Person*. This is what has made it strong, while so much else has proved weak ; that it has a Christ as its middle point, that it has not a circumference without a centre ; that it has not merely deliverance, but a Deliverer ; not redemption only, but a Redeemer as well. This is what makes it fit for wayfaring men. This is what makes it sunlight, and all else, when compared with it, but as moonlight ; fair it may be, but cold and ineffectual, while here the light and the life are one'. And again he says, 'And, oh, how great the difference between submitting ourselves to a complex of rules, and casting ourselves upon a beating heart, between accepting a system, and cleaving to a Person. Our blessedness—and let us not miss it—is, that our treasures are treasured in a Person, who is not for one generation a present Teacher and a living Lord, and then for all succeeding generations a past and a dead one, but who is present and living for all'. Good words, and seasonable words, I judge indeed, I may say these are.

A great combination of like moral glories in the Lord's *ministry* may be traced, as well as in His character. And in ministry we may look at Him in relation to *God*, to *Satan*, and to *man*. As to *God*, the Lord Jesus, in His own Person and ways, was always representing man to God, as God would have him. He was rendering back human nature as a sacrifice of rest, or of sweet savour, as incense pure and fragrant, as a sheaf of untainted first-fruits out of the human soil. He restored to God His complacency in man, which sin or Adam had taken from Him. God's repentance that He had made man (Gen. 6 : 6) was exchanged for delight and glory in man again. And this offering was made to God in the midst of all contradictions, all opposing circumstances, sorrows, fatigues, necessities, and heart-breaking disappointments. Wondrous altar! wondrous offering! A richer sacrifice it infinitely was, than an eternity of Adam's innocency would have been. And He was thus representing man to God, so was He representing God to man.

Through Adam's apostasy, God had been left without an image here ; but now He gets a fuller, brighter image of Himself than Adam could ever have presented. Jesus was letting, not a fair creation, but a ruined, worthless world—know what God was, representing Him in grace, and saying, "He that hath seen me hath seen the *Father*". He declared God. All that is of God, all that can be known of "the light" which no man can approach unto, has now passed before us in Jesus.

And again in the ministry of Christ, looked at in relation to God, we find Him ever mindful of God's rights, ever faithful to God's truth and principles, while in the daily, unwearied actions of relieving man's necessities. Let human sorrow address Him with what appeal it may, He never sacrificed or surrendered any thing that was God's to it. "Glory to God in the highest", was heard over Him at His birth, as well as, "on earth good-will to man"; and according to this God's glory, all through His ministry, was as jealously consulted, as the sinner's need and blessing were diligently served. The echo of those voices, "Glory to God", and "Peace on earth", was, as I may express it heard on every occasion. The Syro-Phoenician's case, already noticed, is a vivid sample of this. Till she took her place in relation to God's purposes and dispensations, He could do nothing for her ; but then, everything.

Surely these are glories in the ministry of the Lord Jesus, in the relations of that ministry to God.

Then as to *Satan*. In the first place, and seasonably

and properly so, the Lord meets him as a *tempter*. Satan sought in the wilderness to impregnate Him with those moral corruptions which he had succeeded in implanting in Adam and the human nature. This victory over the tempter was the needed righteous introduction to all His works and doings touching him. It was, therefore, the Spirit that led Him up to this action. As we read, "Then was Jesus led up of the Spirit into the wilderness, to be tempted of the devil". Ere the Son of God could go forth and spoil the house of the strong man, He must bind him. (Matt. 12 : 29.) Ere He could "reprove" the works of darkness, He must show that He had no fellowship with them. (Eph. 5 11.) He must withstand the enemy, and keep Him outside Himself, ere He could enter his kingdom to destroy his works.

Jesus thus *silenced* Satan. He bound him. Satan had to withdraw as a thoroughly defeated tempter. He could not get anything of his into Him ; he rather found that all that was there was of God. Christ kept outside all that which Adam, under a like temptation, had let inside ; and having thus stood the clean thing, He can go, under a perfect *moral* title, to reprove the unclean.

"Skin for skin", the accuser may have to say of another, and like words that charge and challenge the common corrupted nature ; but he had nothing to do, as an accuser of Jesus, before the throne of God. He was silenced.

Thus His relationship to Satan begins. Upon this, He enters his house and spoils his goods. This world is that house, and there the Lord, in His ministry, is seen effacing various and deep expressions of the enemy's strength. Every deaf or blind one healed, every leper cleansed, every work under His repairing hand, of whatsoever sort it was, was this. It was a spoiling of the goods of the strong man in his own house. Having already bound him, He now spoiled his goods. At last he yields to him as the One that had "the power of death". Calvary was the hour of the power of darkness. All Satan's resources were brought up there, and all his subtlety put forth ; but he was overthrown. His captive was his conqueror. By death He destroyed him that had the power of it. He put away sin by the sacrifice of Himself. The head of the serpent was bruised ; as another has said, that 'death and not man was without strength'.

Thus Jesus the Son of God was the *bruiser* of Satan, as before He had been his *binder* and his *spoiler*. But there is another moral glory that is seen to shine in the ministry of Christ, in the relation it bears to Satan. I mean this : *He never allows him to bear witness to Him.* The testimony may be true, and, as we say, flattering, good words and fair words, such as, "I know thee who thou art, the holy One of God", but Jesus suffered him not to speak. For His ministry was as *pure* as it was gracious. He would not be helped in His ministry by that which He came to destroy. He could have no fellowship with darkness, in His service, any more than in His nature. He could not act on expediency, therefore rebuke and silencing of him was the answer he got to his testimony.* Then as to *man*, the moral glories which show themselves in the ministry of the Lord Jesus are bright and excellent indeed.

* As far as the Lord's ministry in the gospel goes in relation to Satan, He is simply, as we have now seen, his binder, his spoiler, his bruiser. In the Apocalypse, we follow Him in further relations to the same adversary. There we see Him "casting him down from heaven" ; then, in due season, "putting him in the bottomless pit" ; and afterwards "leaving him in the lake that burneth with fire and brimstone". (Rev. 12, 20.) We thus track His conquest over him from the wilderness of the temptation to the lake of fire.

He was constantly *relieving and serving* man in all the variety of his misery ; but He was as surely *exposing* him, showing him to have a nature fully departed from God in revolt and apostasy. But further ; He was exercising him. This is much to be considered, though perhaps not so commonly noticed. In His teaching He exercised people in whatever relation to Himself they stood ; disciples or the multitude, or those who brought their sorrows to Him, or those who were friendly, as I may call them, or those who as enemies were withstanding Him. The disciples He was continually putting through exercises of heart or conscience, as He walked with them and taught them. This is so common that it need not be instanced. The multitude who followed Him He would treat likewise. "Hear and understand", He would say to them ; thus exercising their own minds, as He was teaching them.

To some who brought their sorrows to Him He would say, "Believe ye that I can do this ?" or such like words. The Syro-phoenician is an eminent witness to us how He exercised this class of persons.

Addressing the friendly Simon in Luke 7, after telling him the story of the man who had two debtors, "Tell me", says He, "therefore, which of them will love him most ?"

The Pharisees, His unwearied opposers, He was in like manner constantly calling into exercise. And there is such a voice in this, such a witness of what He is. It tells us that He was not performing summary judgment for them, but would fain lead them to repentance : and so, in calling disciples into exercise, He tells us that we learn His lessons only in a due manner, as far as we are drawn out, in some activity of understanding, heart, or conscience, over them.

This exercising of those He was either leading or teaching is surely another of the moral glories which marked His ministry. But further : in His ministry towards man we see Him frequently as a *reprover*, needfully so, in the midst of such a thing as the human family ; but His way in reproving shines with excellency that we may well admire. When He was rebuking the Pharisees, whom *worldliness* had set in opposition to Him, He uses a very solemn form of words : "He that is not with me is against me". But when He is alluding to those who owned Him and loved Him, but who needed further strength of faith or measure of light, so as to be in full company with Him, He spake in other terms : "He that is not against us is for us".

We notice him again in this character in Matt. 20, in the case of the ten and the two brethren. How does He temper His rebuke because of the good and the right that were in those whom He had to rebuke ? And in this He takes a place apart from His heated disciples, who would not have had their two brethren spared in any measure. He patiently sits over the whole material, and separates the precious from the vile that was in it.

So He is heard again as a reprover in the case of John, forbidding any to cast out devils in His name, if they would not walk with them. But at that moment John's spirit had been under chastening. In the light of the Lord's preceding words, he had been making discovery of the mistake he had committed, and he refers to that mistake, though the Lord himself had in no way alluded to it. But this being so, John having already a sense of his mistake, and artlessly letting it tell itself out, the Lord deals with it in the greatest gentleness. (See Luke 9 : 46-50.)

So as to the Baptist : the Lord rebukes him with marked consideration. He was in prison then. What a fact that must have been in the esteem of the Lord at that moment! But he was to be rebuked for having sent a message to his Lord that reproached Him. But the delicacy of the rebuke is beautiful. He returns a message to John which none but John himself could estimate : "Blessed is he whosoever shall not be offended in me". Even John's disciples, who carried the message between him and the Lord, could not have understood this. Jesus would expose John to himself, but neither to his disciples nor to the world.

So further, His rebuke of the two of Emmaüs, and of Thomas after the resurrection, each has its own excellency. Peter, both in Matt. 16 and 17, has to meet rebuke ; but the rebuke is very differently ministered on each occasion.

But all this variety is full of moral beauty ; and we may surely say, whether His style be peremptory or gentle, sharp or considerate ; whether rebuke on His lips be so reduced as to be scarcely rebuke at all, or so heightened as almost to be the language of repulse and disclaimer ; still, when the occasion is weighed, all this variety will be found to be but various perfections. All these His reproofs were "earrings of gold, and ornaments of fine gold", whether hung or not upon "obedient ears". (Prov. 25 : 12.) "Let the righteous smite me ; it shall be a kindness : and let him reprove me ; it shall be an excellent oil, which shall not break my head". (Psalm 141 : 5.) Surely the Lord gave His disciples to prove this.

CONCLUSION

I have now traced some of the features of the moral glory of the Lord Jesus Christ. He represented man to God—man as he ought to be, and God rested in Him.

This moral perfectness of the Man Christ Jesus, and God's acceptance of Him, was signified by the meat-offering, that cake of fine flour, which was baked either in oven, pan, or frying pan, with its oil and its frankincense. (Lev. 2.)

When the Lord Jesus was here, and thus manifested as Man to God, God's delight in Him was ever expressing itself. He grew up before Him in human nature, and in the exhibition of all human virtues ; and He needed nothing at any one moment to commend Him but Himself, just as He was. In His Person and ways man was morally glorified, so that when the end or perfection of His course came, He could go "straightway" to God, as the sheaf of first-fruits of old was taken directly and immediately, just as it was, out of the field, needing no process to fit it for the presence and acceptance of God. (Lev. 23 : 10.) The title of Jesus to glory was a *moral* one. He had a moral right to be glorified ; His title was in Himself. John 13 : 31, 32 is the blessed setting forth of this in its due connexion. "Now is the Son of man glorified", the Lord there says, just as Judas had left the table ; for that action of Judas was the sure precursor of the Lord's being taken by the Jews, and that was the sure precursor of His being put to death by the gentiles. And the cross being the completeness and perfection of the full form of moral *glory in Him*, it was at this moment He utters these words,

"Now is the Son of man glorified". Then He adds, "and God is glorified in him".

God was as perfectly glorified then as the Son of man was, though the glory was another glory. The Son of man was glorified then, by His *completing* that full form of moral beauty which had been shining in Him all through His life. Nothing of it was then to be wanting, as nothing from the beginning up to that late hour had ever mingled with it that was unworthy of it. The hour was then at hand when it was to shine out in the very last ray that was to give it its full brightness. But God was also glorified then, because all that was of Him was either maintained or displayed. His rights were maintained, His goodness displayed. Mercy and truth, righteousness and peace, were alike and equally either satisfied or gratified. God's truth, holiness, love, majesty, and all beside, were magnified in a way, and illustrated in a light, beyond all that could ever have been known of them elsewhere. The cross, as one has said, is the moral wonder of the universe.

But then again the Lord adds, "If God be glorified in him, God shall also glorify him in himself; and shall straightway glorify him". This is His recognition of His own title to personal glory. He had already perfected the full form of *moral* glory through life and in death. He had also vindicated God's glory, as we have seen. Therefore it was but a righteous thing that He should now enter on *His own personal* glory. And this He did when He took His place in heaven, at the right hand of the majesty there, as in company with God Himself, and all at once, or "straightway".

God's work as Creator had been quickly soiled in man's hand. Man had ruined himself ; so that it is written, "God repented that he had made man". (Gen. 6.) A terrible change in the divine mind, since the day when God saw everything that He had made, and, behold, it was very good! (Gen. 1.) But in the Lord Jesus, the divine complacency in man was restored.

This was blessed! and the more acceptable, as we may say, from the previous repentance. It was more than first enjoyment, it was recovery after loss and disappointment ; and that, too, in a way exceeding the first. And as the first man, upon his sin, had been put *outside* creation, as I may say, this Second Man, (being, as He also was, "the Lord from heaven"), upon His glorifying of God, was seated *at the head* of creation, as at the right hand of the majesty on high. Jesus is in heaven as a glorified Man, because here on earth God had been glorified in Him as the obedient One in life and death. He is there indeed in other characters. Surely we know that. He is there as a Conqueror, as an Expectant, as the High Priest in the tabernacle which God has pitched, as our Forerunner, and as the Purger of our sins. But He is there also, in the highest heavens glorified, because in Him God had been here on earth glorified.

Life and glory were His by personal right, and by moral title. One delights to dwell on such a truth, to repeat it again and again. He never forfeited the garden of Eden. Truly indeed did He walk outside it all His days, or amid the thorns and briers, the sorrows and privations, of a ruined world. But this He did in grace. He took such a condition upon Him ; but He was not exposed to it. He was not, like Adam, like us all, on one side of the cherubim and the flaming sword, and the tree of life and the garden of Eden, on the other. In His history, instead of angels keeping Him outside or beyond the gate, when He had gone through His temptation, they come and minister to Him. For He stood where Adam failed and fell. Therefore, Man as he was, verily and simply Man, He was this distinguished Man. God was glorified in Him, as in all beside He had been dishonoured and disappointed.

In one sense, this perfectness of the Son of man, this moral perfectness, is all for us. It lends its savour to the blood which atones for our sins. It was as the cloud of incense, which went in to the presence of God, together with the blood, on the day of atonement. (Lev. 16.)

But, in another sense, this perfection is too much for us. It is high, we cannot attain to it. It overwhelms the moral sense, as far as we look at it in the recollection of what we *ourselves* are, while it fills us with admiration, as far as we look at it as telling us what *He* is. The personal judicial glory, when displayed of old, was overwhelming. The most favoured of the children of men could not stand before it, as Isaiah, Ezekiel, and Daniel ; and Peter and John experienced the same. And this moral glory, in like manner exposing us, is overwhelming.

Faith, however, is at home in the presence of it. The god of this world blinds the mind to the apprehension and joy of it ; but faith welcomes it. Such are the histories of it here among men. In the presence of it, Pharisees and Sadducees together asked for a sign from heaven. The

mother, through vanity, mistakes it, and the brethren of
the Lord through worldliness. (John 2 : 7.) Disciples
themselves are under constant rebuke from it. The oil
olive beaten for this light was too pure for any ; but it was
ever burning in the sanctuary, or "before the Lord". The
synagogue at Nazareth strikingly lets us learn the unpre-
paredness of man for it. They owned the gracious words
which proceeded out of the Lord's lips ; they felt the
power of them. But quickly a strong current of nature's
corruption set in and withstood this movement in their
hearts, and overcame it. God's humbled, self-emptied
witness, in the midst of a proud, revolted world, was
discovered ; and this would not do for them. Let
"Joseph's son" speak as He may, good words and comfort-
able words, He will not be accepted—He is a carpenter's son.
(Luke 4.) It is wonderful — wonderful witness of the deep
inlaid corruption. Man has his amiabilities, his taste, his
virtues, his sensibilities, as this scene at Nazareth in
Luke 4 may tell us. The gracious words of Jesus raised
a current of good feeling for a moment ; but what was it
all, and where was it all, when God tested it ? Ah ! beloved,
we may still say, in spite of this, our amiability and res-
pectability, our taste and emotions, that in us (that is, in
our flesh) "dwelleth no good thing".

But again, I say, faith is at home with Jesus. Can we,
I ask, treat such an One with fear or suspicion ? Can we
doubt Him ? Could we have taken a distant place from
Him who sat at the well with the woman of Sychar ? Did
she herself take such a place ? Surely, beloved, we should
seek intimacy with Him. The disciples, who companied
with Him, have to learn their lessons again and again. We

know something of this. They had to make discovery of Him afresh, instead of enjoying Him as already discovered. In the 14th of Matthew they had to cry out, "Of a truth, thou art the Son of God". This was discovering Him afresh. Had their faith been simple, they would have slept in the boat with Him. What a scene it was, to their shame and His glory! They spoke insultingly or reproachfully to the Lord, as though He were indifferent to their danger : "Master, carest thou not that we perish?" He awoke at the sound of their voice, and at once set them in safety. But then, He rebukes them, not however for the injustice their hard words had done Him, but for their want of faith.

How perfect was this! How perfect, surely, was everything ; and each in its generation!—the human virtues, the fruits of the anointing that was on Him, and His divine glories. The natures in the One Person are unconfused ; but the effulgence of the divine is chastened, the homeliness of the human is elevated. There is nothing like this, there could be nothing like this, in the whole creation. And yet the human was human, and the divine was divine. Jesus slept in the boat : He was Man. Jesus quelled the winds and the waves : He was God.

This moral glory must shine. Other glories must give place till this is done. The Greeks, who had come to worship in Jerusalem at the feast, enquire after Jesus, desiring to see Him. This savoured of the kingdom, or of the royal glory of the Messiah. It was a sample of that day, when the nations shall come up to the city of the Jews, to keep holy day ; and when, as King in Zion, He shall be Lord of all, and God of the whole earth.

But there was a secret deeper than this. It needs a juster sense of God's way, than simply to be expecting a kingdom. The Pharisees needed that, when in Luke 17 they asked the Lord when the kingdom should appear. He had to tell them of another kingdom, which they did not apprehend—a kingdom *within*, a present kingdom, which had to be entered and known, ere the glorious manifested kingdom could appear. The disciples needed it in Acts 1, when they asked their Lord if He would at that time restore the kingdom to Israel. He had to tell them also of another thing, ere the restoration could take place ; that they were to be gifted by the Spirit, for testimony to Him all the world over.

So here in John 12. The Lord lets us know that *moral glory* must precede the kingdom. He will surely shine in the glory of the throne by and by, and the gentiles shall then come to Zion, and see the King in His beauty ; but ere that could be, the moral glory must be displayed in all its fulness and unsulliedness. And this was His thought now, when the gentiles had inquired after Him. "The hour is come that the Son of man should be glorified". This was His moral glory, as we have said before, in John 13 : 31, 32. It had been shining all through His ways, from His birth hitherto ; His death was to be the completeness of it ; and therefore the hour was then at hand, when it was to shine out in the last ray that was to form it, and give it perfection. The Lord thus supplies or introduces on this occasion, as He did, as we have seen, in Luke 17 and in Acts 1, the truth, the additional truth, which needs the richer, juster sense of God's ways to apprehend. The moral glory must be fully displayed, ere Messiah can show Himself in royal glory to the ends of the earth.

It is, however, His, and His only. How infinitely distant from one's heart is any other thought! When the heavens opened, in Acts 10, the sheet was seen descending ere Peter was commanded to have fellowship with it, or ere it ascended and was lost or hid again on high. The contents of it had to be cleansed or sanctified. But when the heaven was opened in Matt. 3, Jesus on earth needed not to be taken up to be approved there, but voices and visions from on high sealed and attested Him just as He was. "This is my beloved Son, in whom I am well pleased."

And when the heavens were opened again, as in Matt. 27, that is, when the vail of the temple was rent in twain, all was finished, nothing more was needed, the work of Jesus was sealed and attested just as it then was. An opened heaven at the beginning shone out in the full acceptance of His *Person* ; an opened heaven at the end shone out in full acceptance of His *work*.

And let me close in saying, that it is blessed and happy, as well as part of our worship, to mark the characteristics of the Lord's way and ministry here on the earth, as I have been seeking in measure to do in this paper ; for all that He did and said, all His service, whether in the substance or the style of it, is the witness of what He was, and He is the witness to us of what God is. And thus we reach God, the blessed One, through the paths of the Lord Jesus, in the pages of the evangelists. Every step of that way becomes important to us. All that He did and said was a real, truthful expression of Himself, as He Himself was a

real, truthful expression of God. And if we can understand the character of His ministry, or read the moral glory
that attaches to each moment and each particular of His
walk and service here on earth, and so learn what He is,
and thus learn what God is, we reach God, in certain and
unclouded knowledge of Him, through the ordinary paths
and activities of the life of this divine Son of man.

———